LIGHT
LOOK OUT!

Wendy Sadler

Raintree

Chicago, Illinois

Printed by South China Printing Company

10 09 08 07 06
10 9 8 7 6 5 4 3 2 1

Library of Congress Cataloging-in-Publication Data
Sadler, Wendy.
  Light : look out! / Wendy Sadler.
    p. cm. -- (Science in your life)
  Includes bibliographical references and index.
  ISBN 1-4109-1551-4 (library binding-hardcover) --
ISBN 1-4109-1559-X (pbk.)
 1. Light--Juvenile literature. 2. Color--Juvenile
literature. 3. Reflection (Optics)--Juvenile literature.
I. Title.
  QC360.S23 2006
  535--dc22

                    2005014637

Acknowledgments
Alamy Images pp. 16 (BananaStock), 11
(Brand X Pictures), 14 (GOODSHOOT), 17
(Momentum Creative Group), 19 (Nick Hanna),
21 (The National Trust Photolibrary); Corbis
pp. 25 (LWA-Sharle Kennedy), 12 (Koopman);
Corbis Royalty Free pp. 15, 22, 26; Getty Images
pp. 5, 6, 20, 23 (PhotoDisc); Harcourt Education Ltd
pp. 8, 9, 27 (Tudor Photography); Photographers
Direct pp. 4 (Antoinette Burton), 24 (Life File Photos
Ltd), 10 (Lightphotographic); Photolibrary.com/ Ips
co Ltd p.13; Science Photo Library p. 18 (Tony
McConnell); SeaPics.com p. 7 (Mick McMurray).

Cover photograph of fireworks reproduced with
permission of Getty/BrandX.

Every effort has been made to contact copyright
holders of any material reproduced in this book.
Any omissions will be rectified in subsequent
printings if notice is given to the publishers.

The paper used to print this book comes from
sustainable resources.

Disclaimer
All the Internet addresses (URLs) given in this book
were valid at the time of going to press. However,
due to the dynamic nature of the Internet, some
addresses may have changed, or sites may have
changed or ceased to exist since publication. While
the author and publishers regret any inconvenience
this may cause readers, no responsibility for any
such changes can be accepted by either the author
or the publishers.

An adult should supervise all of the activities in
this book.

Contents

Any words appearing in the text in bold, **like this**, are explained in the glossary.

Light Is All Around You

Light really is all around you! Light helps you find your way around, indoors and out. It helps you see shapes and colors when you are playing games. The numbers on a clock can light up to tell you the time when it is dark. The morning sunlight tells you it soon will be time to get up.

When the Sun comes up, it is nearly time to wake up.

Light in your life!

Look at this list of things you might have done today that used light:

- switched on the bathroom light
- read a comic or a book
- looked at the time
- looked in the mirror.

Which of these have you done? Can you think of any more things you have done that used light?

Could you catch a ball in the dark?

Where Does Light Come From?

Most light that we use comes from things that are very, very hot. When you are outside in the daytime you can see things because of the light coming from the Sun. The Sun is very hot, and this is why it gives out a lot of light. At nighttime, when we do not have the light from the Sun, it is dark outside.

When something gets very hot, it starts to glow. This glow gives off light. First it glows a red color, and then as it gets hotter it becomes white.

The wire in a light bulb is called a filament. When it gets hot, it glows very brightly.

Some things give off light without getting hot. The light and colors on your television screen come from special **chemicals** that glow when given **electricity**.

Other lights, such as the ones in clock radios, are called **light-emitting diodes**, or LEDs for short. LEDs also use electricity to make light, and they do not get hot.

Some jellyfish in the deep, dark parts of the sea can make their own light by mixing special chemicals in their body.

How Does Light Travel?

Light travels in straight lines called rays. You can tell this by looking at shadows. Shadows are formed by objects that block light rays from passing through. If you put one of these objects between a light and a wall, you can make a shadow on the wall.

You can use your hands to make shadow shapes on the wall because light cannot go through your hands.

Light travels very, very quickly. A ray of light could travel around the world in less than one second! When you switch on a light, you cannot see it move from the light bulb to your eyes because it happens much too quickly.

Light bends when it travels from one type of **material** into another. If a ray of light travels through water and then air, the light bends. This is because air is a gas and water is a liquid.

Light in your life!

Put a spoon into a glass of water. The spoon looks bent, but it is the light that is bending as it goes from the water to the air.

Light the Messenger

Light is used to send messages because it travels so quickly. Traffic lights use colored lights to send a message. Red lights tell you when to stop, and green lights tell you when to go.

These traffic lights help keep the traffic moving safely and smoothly by using light to send messages.

Light can be made to go around corners using something called an **optical fiber**. This special **material** is as thin as one of the hairs on your head! The light travels along the optical fiber and carries messages with it.

Light travels to the end of these optical fibers to make this lamp sparkle.

Light in your life!

Get a flashlight and use it to send a message to a friend without using your voice or a pen and paper! Use Morse code, which uses long and short flashes to send a message. A dot (.) is a short flash and a dash (–) is a long flash. Each letter of the alphabet has its own code. Try sending this message:

. . . – – – . . .

This message means S.O.S (save our souls), and it can be used to call for help. You can find the full Morse code on page 28. Can you send your own message?

Reflection

When light hits an object, some of the light will usually bounce off. When light bounces off something, it is called a **reflection**. Hard and shiny objects are very good at reflecting light.

A mirror is made of glass and metal. The metal is very shiny, so it reflects light well. Without a mirror you could not check your hair in the morning!

The tiny mirrors on this ball reflect light in many directions.

Most objects that we see every day do not give off any light of their own. We see these objects because the light that comes from the Sun or a light bulb reflects off of them. The light bouncing off the objects travels into our eyes. When the light reaches our eyes, we can see the objects.

The knives and forks on this table are made of shiny metal and reflect a lot of light.

Mirror, Mirror on the Wall

A mirror is a very **reflective** object that lets you see what you look like. Light bounces off your face and hits the mirror. The light then bounces back off the mirror and toward your eyes, and you see your face.

A dentist uses a small mirror to look at your teeth. By holding the mirror at an angle, the dentist can get the light from the back of your mouth to bounce up toward his or her eyes.

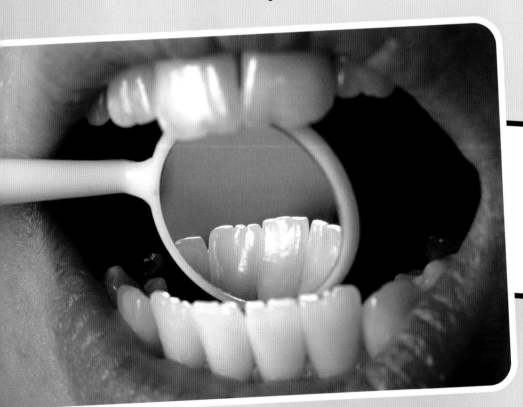

This mirror helps the dentist see the back of the teeth.

The mountains are reflected in the still waters of the lake. That is why you see them twice.

Water can make good reflections, too. If you look at a puddle or a lake, you can sometimes see a reflection of the sky. The smooth **surface** of the water is a bit like a mirror. If it is windy and the water has ripples, then the light will not reflect as well off the surface.

How Do We See?

Our eyes take in light from things around us. Some things, such as light bulbs and television screens, give off their own light. Most things we see do not make their own light. Instead, they **reflect** light that comes from other places.

At the back of your eye there are some special **cells** that **react** to light. These cells build up a pattern of the colors you are seeing. The pattern made at the back of the eye is sent to your brain. Your brain figures out what the pattern is. Without your brain, your eyes would not be able to see anything!

There are **muscles** in your eyes that can move your eyes in the direction of the thing you want to see. The pupils are the black parts of your eyes. Light enters your eyes through the pupils.

When you are in a dark room, your pupil gets very large to let in as much light as possible. In a bright place, the pupil gets much smaller.

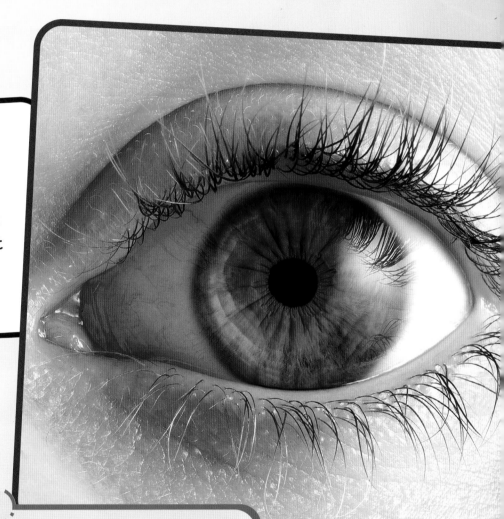

Light in your life!

Ask a friend to try to move their eyes smoothly from left to right. Look at their eyes while they do it. Do the eyes move smoothly? Now move your finger from left to right and ask your friend to follow it with their eyes. Now do the eyes move smoothly?

Invisible Light

There are some types of light that our eyes cannot see. When you turn on the television with a remote control, you are using a type of light called **infrared**. Heat from the Sun, and from our bodies, can also make infrared light.

This picture was taken using a special camera that can pick up infrared light and turn it into a picture.

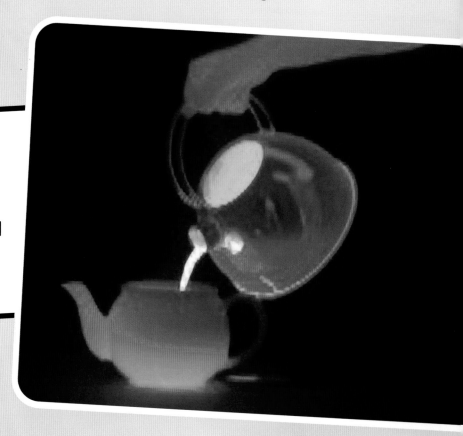

Firefighters can use special cameras that pick up the invisible light and turn it into a picture. This means that they can find people in the dark, or if they are trapped underground.

Another type of invisible light is called **ultraviolet**. This light comes from the Sun, and it can give you sunburn. Sunscreen is used to block the ultraviolet, or UV, light so that it does not reach your skin.

You should put sunscreen on any areas of skin that are not covered by clothes to protect yourself from ultraviolet light.

What Is Color?

White light is a mixture of all the colors in a **rainbow**. You can use a triangle-shaped piece of glass to split up the light into all the separate colors. The glass shape is called a **prism**.

Rainbows appear when rain and sunshine happen at the same time. The light from the Sun goes through the raindrops and splits up into all the colors, like passing through a prism. When these colors reach your eye, you see the rainbow.

The colors in the light bend as they travel through the glass. Blue bends more than red, so the colors all split up.

Some windows have lots of different colors in them. They are called stained glass windows.

When an object looks red, this is because it takes in all the other colors in white light except red. We say that it **absorbs** the other colors. The red is **reflected** into our eyes, so we see red.

If light is shining through a window, you can make colors by using colored glass. Blue glass will block all the other colors except blue. This means you see blue light shining through that part of the window.

Chemical Colors

Some **chemicals** give off colored light when they get very hot. Street lights sometimes shine with a yellow-orange light because of a chemical called sodium. When sodium gets hot, it glows a yellow-orange color.

Fireworks come in lots of different colors. They are made by mixing different chemicals together. When the fireworks burn, they give off colored light. Fireworks are very dangerous, and you should never play with them!

Different chemicals in the fireworks give us displays of different colored lights.

A telescope collects light from objects in the sky, so you can see them more clearly.

Astronomers are scientists who look up at the sky to find out more about space, the stars, and the planets. They can look at the colors of the stars in the sky and figure out what chemicals they are made of. Astronomers use special telescopes to help them see the stars.

Energy from Light

Light has **energy**. We can use the energy from light to heat things. Dark-colored objects are very good at **absorbing** the heat from light. Light-colored objects do not absorb as much heat.

If you put water into a dark-colored container on a sunny day, it gets hot. This is called **solar** heating. Solar is a word that means "to do with the Sun."

Solar panels can turn energy from the Sun into electricity. You can sometimes see these on the roofs of houses.

Green plants take in light from the Sun and turn it into energy to make them grow. People and animals eat the plants to get energy. This means that we all get our energy from the Sun. We are all solar powered!

We get our energy by eating food. The energy in the food has come from the Sun because sunlight helped the plants grow.

What Is a Laser?

A laser is a special type of light that shines with just one color. A laser has a thin beam of light that can be very powerful.

The laser beam at a supermarket checkout reads the pattern of lines printed on the package or can of food. This pattern is called a bar code. The pattern gives the price and also tells the shop what you have bought.

A laser reads the bar code and enters the price of the item.

Light is used all around you in many ways. Without it we would not be able to see ourselves in a mirror, play music on our compact disc, or CD, player, or see the colors of the world around us. Use your eyes to find other ways that we use light every day.

Inside a CD player a laser beam reads a pattern of tiny holes on the surface of the disc. The pattern of holes is turned into music!

Facts About Light

Try sending your own messages using Morse **code**. All you need is a flashlight. Remember that a dot (.) is a short flash and a dash (—) is a long flash.

A	.—	S	...
B	—...	T	—
C	—.—.	U	..—
D	—..	V	...—
E	.	W	.——
F	..—.	X	—..—
G	——.	Y	—.——
H	....	Z	——..
I	..	0	—————
J	.———	1	.————
K	—.—	2	..———
L	.—..	3	...——
M	——	4	....—
N	—.	5	.....
O	———	6	—....
P	.——.	7	——...
Q	——.—	8	———..
R	.—.	9	————.

Thomas Edison invented the light bulb in 1879, more than 100 years ago!

A light year is a way of measuring really big distances. A light year is the distance that light would travel in 1 year. A light year is 6 trillion miles.

Light takes about 8 seconds to get to us from the Sun.

X-rays are a type of light. X-rays can go through your body, but not through your bones. Doctors can use them to see inside you and check for broken bones.

Energy-efficient light bulbs use a quarter of the energy of ordinary light bulbs— and they last up to 20 times longer!

Find Out More

You can find out more about science in everyday life by talking to your teacher or parents. Your local library will also have books that can help. You will find the answers to many of your questions in this book. If you want to know more, you can use other books and the Internet.

More books to read

Cooper, Chris. *Science Answers: Light*. Chicago: Heinemann Library, 2003.

Hunter, Rebecca. *Discovering Science: Light and Dark*. Chicago: Raintree, 2003.

Parker, Steve. *Science Files: Light*. Chicago: Heinemann Library, 2004.

Using the Internet

Explore the Internet to find out more about light. Try using a search engine such as www.yahooligans.com or www.internet4kids.com, and type in keywords such as "**LED**," "**optical fiber**," and "**prism**."

Glossary

absorbs takes in. Some objects absorb light.

astronomer someone who studies space, the stars, and the planets

cell very tiny unit that makes up all living things. Different cells in the body do different jobs.

chemical kind of substance. Everything around us is made of chemicals.

code way of sending messages using numbers, letters, or shapes

electricity form of energy that can be used to make things run. Computers and televisions run using electricity.

energy power to make things work. You need energy to get up and walk or run around.

filament thin piece of wire that gets hot and glows inside a light bulb

infrared light that we cannot see with our eyes. Infrared light is used in television remote controls.

light-emitting diode type of light that glows when electricity goes through it. Its short form is LED.

material something that objects are made from

muscle part of the body that helps us move around

optical fiber thin thread that light signals move along

prism triangle-shaped piece of glass that can be used to show all the colors of the rainbow

rainbow when all the colors in light are split up so you can see them

react do or change something. If you react to light, the light is a signal that makes you do something.

reflect bounce off

reflection when light bounces off a surface

solar from the Sun

surface top or outside part of an object

ultraviolet light that you cannot see. Ultraviolet light from the Sun can give you sunburn.

Index